Be a Good Leader!

Jennifer Overend Prior, Ph.D.

Consultants

Shelley Scudder
Gifted Education Teacher
Broward County Schools

Caryn Williams, M.S.Ed.
Madison County Schools
Huntsville, AL

Publishing Credits

Dona Herweck Rice, *Editor-in-Chief*
Lee Aucoin, *Creative Director*
Torrey Maloof, *Editor*
Diana Kenney, M.A.Ed., NBCT, *Associate Education Editor*
Marissa Rodriguez, *Designer*
Stephanie Reid, *Photo Editor*
Rachelle Cracchiolo, M.S.Ed., Publisher

Image Credits: Cover, pp. 1, 9 Alamy; p. 19 Corbis; pp. 12, 13, 16–17, 18, 24 Getty Images; pp. 4, 5, 8, 10 iStockphoto; p. 14 The Library of Congress [3a17019u]; p. 6 The Library of Congress [LC-DIG-pga-03757]; p. 11 The Library of Congress [LC-DIG-ppmsca-19241]; p. 15 The Library of Congress [LC-DIG-det-4a27975]; p. 7 The White House; All other images from Shutterstock.

Teacher Created Materials
5301 Oceanus Drive
Huntington Beach, CA 92649-1030
http://www.tcmpub.com

ISBN 978-1-4333-6973-5

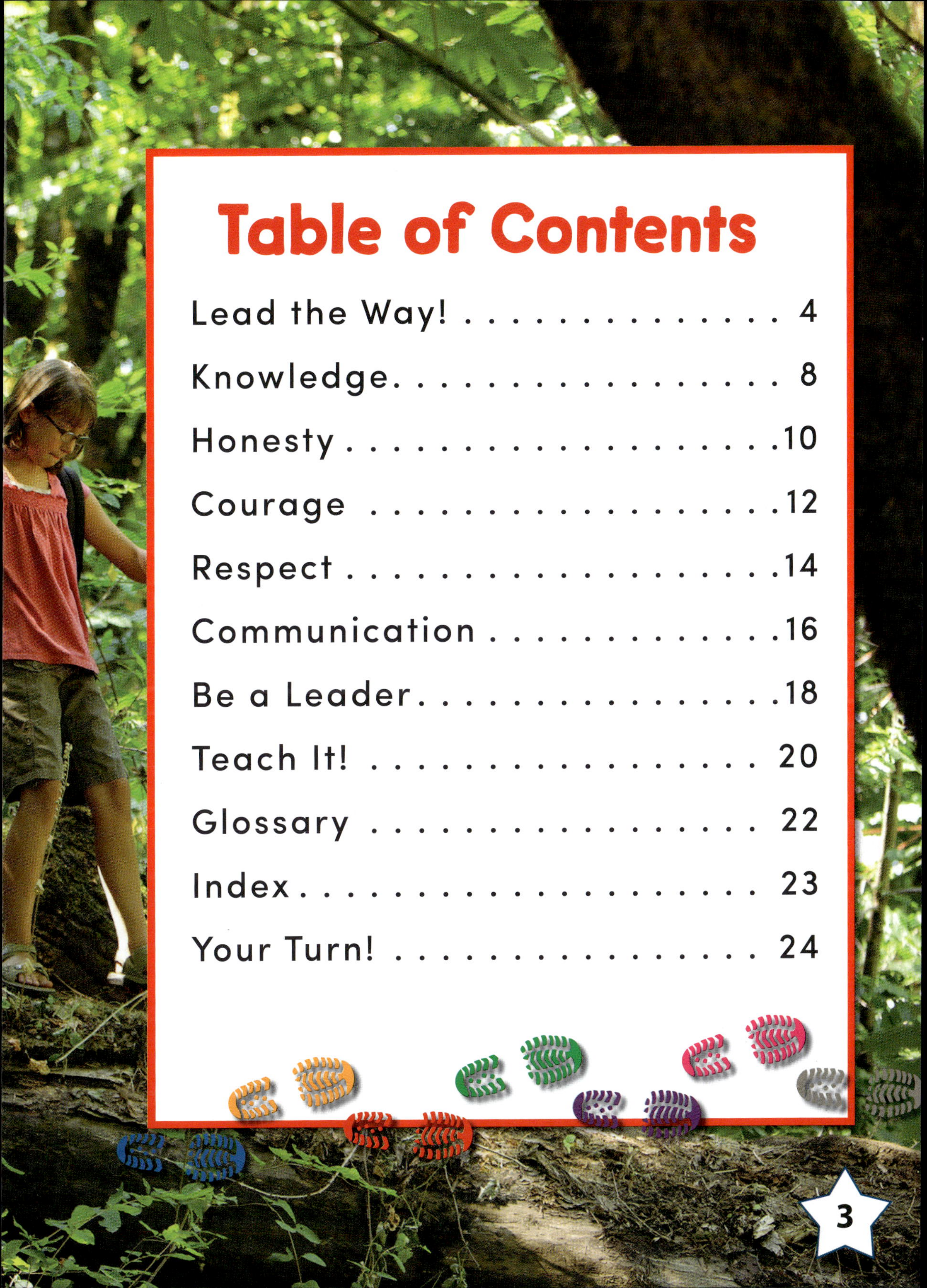

Table of Contents

Lead the Way! 4

Knowledge. 8

Honesty 10

Courage 12

Respect 14

Communication 16

Be a Leader. 18

Teach It! 20

Glossary 22

Index. 23

Your Turn! 24

Lead the Way!

What is a **leader**? Do you know? A leader guides people. A leader is helpful and fair.

This soccer coach leads his team.

This girl gets a star for leading her troop.

Leaders think about what is best. Then they help make choices for the group. Good leaders show people the way.

George Washington was a good leader. He was the first president of the United States.

The President

The president of the United States is a leader. The president leads the country.

President Barack Obama

Knowledge

Good leaders are smart. They know how to make good choices. Leaders have **knowledge** (NOL-ij) to share.

These parents share knowledge with their kids.

Many Leaders

Parents are leaders in families. Teachers are leaders in schools.

This teacher shares knowledge with a student.

Honesty

A good leader is **honest** (ON-ist). Leaders should tell the truth. People should be able to trust leaders.

Judges are leaders in a courtroom.

Honest Abe

Abraham Lincoln (LING-kuhn) was a president of the United States. People say he told the truth. They called him Honest Abe.

Abraham Lincoln

Courage

A leader has **courage** (KUR-ij). You have courage when you do the right thing even if you are scared.

Astronauts show courage when they travel to space.

Soldiers show courage when they go to war.

Respect

A good leader shows **respect** (ri-SPEKT). Good leaders also earn respect. They can earn it by being fair and **polite**.

Alexander Graham Bell earned respect when he invented the telephone.

Earn It!

Leaders also earn respect by having good ideas.

A man uses the first telephone.

Communication

Good leaders know how to **communicate** (kuh-MYOO-ni-keyt) well. They have good writing **skills**. They speak clearly. They listen carefully.

This father speaks to his son.

Speak Up!

Good leaders make sure people can hear them loudly and clearly.

Dr. Martin Luther King Jr. speaks to a crowd.

Be a Leader

You can be a leader! You can be a leader at home. You can be a leader at school.

This girl leads the Pledge of Allegiance.

This boy leads his team.

Teach It!

Be a leader. Teach a friend a new game. Be honest about the rules. Talk about what your friend did well.

This girl teaches her friend how to play a new game.

This boy teaches his friend how to play chess.

Glossary

communicate—to give information about something to someone else

courage—the ability to do the right thing even if you are scared

honest—truthful

knowledge—information you get from learning things

leader—someone who guides other people

polite—having good manners

respect—the way you show that someone or something is important

skills—things you do well

Index

Bell, Alexander Graham, 14

courage, 12–13

King, Dr. Martin Luther Jr., 17

knowledge, 8–9

Lincoln, Abraham, 11

Obama, Barack, 7

respect, 14–15

Washington, George, 6

Your Turn!

Lead the Way

The girl in the photo leads the Pledge of Allegiance. What are some ways you can be a leader at school? How do you feel when you are a leader? Write about you as a leader.